Writing
Exercises

· ·

How to Teach Writing and
Prepare Your Favorite Students
for College, Life and
Everything Else

Ed Newman

For Susie.
A truly great homeschool teacher.

Table of Contents

Introduction

*"Since attention follows interest, it is folly
to attempt to gain attention without first stimulating interest."*

– John Milton Gregory, The Seven Laws of Teaching

Like many American boys, I grew up playing baseball, football and basketball. We had pickup games throughout the year and intramurals at school. Many of us even earned our varsity letters in one sport or another.

With the exception of California there were few, if any, varsity soccer teams when I grew up. So it was an interesting experience becoming a soccer coach when my son took an interest in this exhilarating sport at age six or seven. I believe his first attraction was the international character of the game. Soccer cards depict every nationality and the corresponding flags of a multitude of nations.

Though I had only a modest relationship with soccer, I accepted the responsibilities of coaching and determined to excel at it. To do this I did what I usually do: I visited our local library and found books on the game. I studied the drills and exercises to develop my players' skills. And I learned the rules.

I also attended a clinic for coaches led by Buzz Lagos, head coach of the Minnesota Thunder professional soccer team. It was from Mr. Lagos, or "Coach" as he preferred to be called, that I learned what I consider to be the most important principle for writing teachers.

Coach Lagos and several players from the Thunder conducted the clinic.

During the clinic we spent most of our time playing various games designed to teach soccer skills and develop our awareness of key principles. At the end of the evening we then gathered for a question-and-answer period.

During this Q&A one of my fellow coaches asked a question that was undoubtedly a burning issue for a number of us. "Sir, what skill level should my kids be at when they are 10 years old?" Here it was. What are the benchmarks that our boys and girls should aspire to as they advance in age? How deft should their ball handling be? How strong and true should they be kicking? How skilled in passing and receiving? How effective their ball control and other maneuvers?

Coach Lagos stunned me with his answer. He said, "Don't even think about it. Only one thing is important--that they enjoy the game."

Interesting answer.

We all know it's true. The key to success in any endeavor is motivation. And that's how our kids are going to become great writers, not by being forced to write but by learning to enjoy it.

Your student or child will write more if she enjoys it rather than hates it. Think about it. The more they write, the more sentences and words you'll have to edit. You'll also gain insights into your child's thinking. You'll receive glimpses of who your students and children really are.

Though I created the following exercises to be fun, their aims are serious. Kids will learn not simply to write in sentences. Rather, they'll learn some of the methods professional writers use to create interesting sentences. Kids will learn how to use the tools that help professionals to become better writers.

Good writing is more than simply writing technically correct sentences with proper verb tense and punctuation. **Good writing is writing that engages readers.**

I strongly believe that learning how to communicate by means of the written word is a key component of any successful career. Kids who become good writers will obtain more career opportunities and find more open doors than those who neglect this vital skill.

. . . .

Do you remember the first time a professional carpenter showed you how to hold a hammer and pound a nail? Don't hold the hammer in the middle. You hold it at the end of the handle and let the head of the hammer do the work. A neat trick, eh? It makes a difference in the results you get — fewer bent nails, less frustration, and a generally more pleasurable experience.

So, too, with writing. Once your kids learn a few tricks, they'll have fewer bent nails, less frustration, and a generally more pleasurable writing experience. One aim of this book, therefore, is to help teachers give their students this pleasurable scholastic experience. Writing does not have to be a drag.

. . . .

These exercises are best suited for junior high and early high school students. But your children – whether younger or older – can benefit as well. This book does not promise to be an end-all be-all set of exercises to teach students everything they'll ever need to know to become great writers. I can guarantee, however, that as you work your way through these writing exercises and implement the teaching method I propose, your child or student will become a better writer as a result.

This is not a comprehensive writing book. It is, however, a valid tool. How far you run with it is up to you.

How this book is laid out.

The aim of this book is to arm parents and teachers with a philosophical approach to teaching writing skills along with exercises to help implement it. The three goals of this method and the accompanying exercises are:

- To build students' confidence as writers.
- To improve students' creative thinking through creative writing prompts.
- To provide useful strategies for teaching invaluable writing skills such as grammar, punctuation and techniques to add interest to students' writing.

Chapter 1 underscores the importance of writing. Learning to write is not simply for professional writers. Writing well increases one's value in nearly any occupation, especially in our communications age. Chapter 2 addresses practical matters for getting started. Chapter 3 talks about the writer's notebooks, why they are important and how they help. In chapter 4 we address handwriting. It seems archaic, but we'll learn there's value in good handwriting. Chapter 5 addresses research skills, chapter 6 deals with the matter of attribution, and chapter 7 discusses the young writer's schedule as well as the teacher's. In chapter 8 I share my approach to grading, an aspect of the process that is of utmost importance. Teachers serve as collaborators in the grading/correction process. Chapter 9 addresses a few of the more subtle aspects of writing along with techniques to which the pros pay attention.

Part II contains the writing exercises. As already noted, this is not a comprehensive writing course. It is aimed at improving students' approach to writing and helping them think more broadly about writing while providing techniques for improving their written communication skills.

. . . .

Key Concepts from this Intro

1. Create better writers by making writing fun.
2. Children who are better writers experience more career opportunities and open doors.
3. Good writing engages readers.
4. Learning a few tricks and techniques can make a big difference in your students' writing success.

PART I:
The Setup

Chapter 1: The importance of Writing

Writing has changed the world more than almost any other activity. Truth is passed on from one generation to the next through the written word.

Political movements may begin with a fire in the breast, but it is the written word that distributes this fire far and wide. The American Revolution was successful in large part because of the printing press. The sacred truths of Judaism, Christianity, Buddhism, Hinduism and Islam have influence because their holy books have been preserved in writing.

Why do we remember Marco Polo's travels to China but know nothing of his uncle's previous journeys to this exotic foreign land? The answer is self-evident when we learn that Marco Polo spent time in prison with a writer who recorded his stories and preserved them for posterity.

In the business world, it is almost impossible to be a person of influence without writing skills. Whether crafting business plans or sales presentations, memos or ad copy, the written word is the coin of the realm.

For the most part our young peoples' future influence will be in direct proportion to their skill with the written word.

Chapter 2: Getting Started

> "Do not deny yourself the help of good books on the subject
> of your lessons. Buy, borrow, or beg, if necessary,
> but obtain somehow the help of the best thinkers..."
>
> – John Milton Gregory, *The Seven Laws of Teaching*

In our home my wife carried the primary burden of choosing curricula, preparing lessons, establishing routines, maintaining transcripts and most of the other major roles in the education of our children. Being a professional writer myself it only seemed natural that I'd get involved in this area. In addition to writing instruction, I kept tabs on our kids' progress by creating tests, occasionally reviewing their work and updating report cards.

These years were an ongoing learning experience for all of us. As a homeschool educator Susie read seemingly countless books on education, many of which she shared with me. If you aim to be a homeschool instructor, I strongly recommend this habit of being a lifelong learner yourself.

Not every book is for every person. That's O.K. Your own pupils will have the same experience with some of their own reading materials, whether at home or in public school. You can help them develop the habit of critical thinking as well as learning how to glean what has value, or as we used to say, "Eat the meat and spit out the bones."

I should note a few practical matters. First, get yourself some fine-point red pens for grading. The extra ones will be on hand so you're not stuck if you lose the only one in the house. (I personally like the Pilot Precise V5, Extra Fine.) Second, make sure you're capable of grading the work by having a firm grasp of spelling and grammar yourself. If you are weak in this area, bone up by studying Strunk & White's *Elements of Style*. Don't neglect the other reference books cited in the appendix.

Chapter 3: The Writer's Notebooks

It is my recommendation that each student have their own personal "writer's notebook" in which he or she has all homework in one place. A spiral-bound notebook with lined paper works best. This notebook should be used only for the writing exercises, no other purpose. While working on later exercises students can review past progress and get reminders from previous lessons. The notebook is an efficient caretaker of the writer's progress.

I know that computers are in most homes these days and kids learn how to do work on the computer at an early age, but it's my opinion that the notebook offers many advantages, not the least of which is helping one to improve penmanship. Nearly every famous writer has carried notebooks for the purpose of capturing ideas and observations much like a butterfly net is used to gather butterflies. The notebook serves as a place to pin the student's work for additional review and offers easy access to evidence of progress.

In no way would we suggest eliminating the use of computers, tablets or the Internet. The National Council of Teachers of English (NCTE) has stressed the importance of becoming proficient with these tools of technology. For the purposes of this book and the method presented here we want to underscore the value of learning to write with pen in hand.

NOTE: It may be that you want each student to have and use two notebooks, one for completed work and a second as a place to capture ideas and observations. Because writing is a personal journey, the second notebook can be taken anywhere in the home and, ideally, become something of a companion to the student.

Learning to write well is essentially an individual process. Each student advances at his or her own rate and experiences his or her own challenges and victories. The writer's notebook serves as a personal reminder of the struggles and the progress, providing a constant resource that can help them in personal ways.

For example, the writer's notebook should be a no-stress zone where the student is free to make mistakes and learn from them. It can contain a list of new vocabulary words, writing brainstorms or the piece of writing of which they're most proud. In fact, the versatility of the contents of the writer's notebook is perhaps its most valuable quality. Each student's notebook will take on the personal characteristics of the student's personal writing journey. The point is, it's useful to keep one's materials in one place where the student can refer to them easily, at any time.

Furthermore, it's valuable to have a writing notebook on hand at all times because writing inspiration often will not wait for the pen/paper/desk/writing hour combination. Instead, most students find that it's most difficult to write when they're faced with a blank piece of paper and the vague directive, "Write something!" Instead, students find inspiration while they're walking the dog, or while finishing homework for another class. Maybe even a discussion over the dinner table will spark the writing inspiration. In these situations, if the student doesn't have a notebook nearby in which to jot their thoughts, the majority of this newfound inspiration will be lost forever.

Chapter 4: Handwriting Matters

This chapter contains some suggestions that may appear contrary to the philosophy of this book: to make learning fun through a personal and creative teaching approach. Hopefully, the tedium of learning good penmanship has already been addressed at an earlier stage in their development. Nevertheless, you'll see here why we underscore good handwriting.

Good handwriting is becoming lost in our modern society. With the advent of online news forums and digital books, print and concrete handwriting skills may seem unnecessary. Computers and other devices are replacing the pen.

Developing good handwriting, however, is still important for a variety of reasons. Good handwriting shows courtesy toward those reading what you write. It's also something of a necessity when filling out a job application. And, if the teacher can't read the pupil's work, then there's going to be a problem when going over it together.

Without even harping on it, as you work with the student to improve her storytelling abilities, handwriting will improve on its own, for two reasons. First, handwriting is a motor skill that improves with use. Second, by being interested in helping her communicate more effectively, the student will take greater care to write more clearly. After all, she may be quite proud of the stories or ideas she is attempting to share and won't intentionally aim to have poor handwriting be an impediment.

Since the beginning of literacy, handwriting proficiency has developed and changed in lockstep with changes in society and technology. Some forms of handwriting are artistic, such as calligraphy or graffiti. Others are more utilitarian, such as the near-illegible scrawl used in a doctor's office. All handwriting, being the medium in which a message is conveyed, is affected by both the writer and the reader. For example, a dinner invitation written in pristine calligraphy will be received differently than one written in a sloppy scrawl. Each note will elicit a different response. While one note may imply a formal dinner with suit and tie, the latter indicates that jeans and a t-shirt will be adequate. In this way, it is important to be aware of handwriting and the affect it has on others.

Furthermore, it is courteous for handwritten messages to be easily legible to the recipient. Your student will likely one day secure a job in which written notes may be a necessity. Handwritten notes are still an important form of communication in most employment settings. For example, you may be a boss scribbling written corrections on a proposal. If your notes can't be accurately interpreted, the proposal may end up conveying misinformation with the result that your company loses an important contract. Developing good handwriting throughout an academic career could be very important in future careers.

Developing good handwriting is also useful in developing linear thinking. When using a computer, it is easy to edit the format of sentences and whole paragraphs with a series of clicks. Word order is entirely flexible. Conversely, handwriting with pen and paper requires the mind to sequentially order the thoughts and plan further ahead when writing, sharpening critical thinking skills. This type of brain development is not present when solely typing on a computer. In fact, it turns out that current brain research is affirming that writing by hand is important.

At the same time, maintaining good handwriting forces students to be disciplined in writing out their ideas. While computers maintain pristine uniformity with absolutely no effort on the part of the writer, precision in handwriting requires both attention and discipline. (This is not to imply that good writing using a computer is effortless. It only resolves the legibility issue.)

In these ways, it is easy to see that handwriting is an important skill to develop in the student. Here are a few tips to help improve handwriting:

1. **Practice.** Begin when your students are young. Our writing exercises here assume the student has already developed a certain measure of legibility. If not, have the student make a conscious effort to improve this skill.

2. **Develop good handwriting muscles.** The muscles that should primarily be used in handwriting are muscles in the forearm and back. Too much finger muscle use in handwriting will produce small, cramped handwriting as the writer painstakingly draws each letter individually.

3. **Strive for uniformity.** The key to good handwriting is consistency. If they really need help in this area it may be necessary to have a separate notebook for the students to practice each letter until they can easily maintain a uniform shape for each. I know it sounds tedious and boring, but there's a lifetime payoff.

. . . .

A Note About Typing Skills

There was a time when literacy was not a necessary survival skill. In today's world, however, reading and writing skills are assumed. Job postings often outline the software programs now required for these openings.

What about typing skills? I recently heard someone say that with the advent of voice-recognition software, typing will become a thing of the past. I'm willing to wager that this won't happen in my lifetime, and it won't happen in your children's either. In a country where we have difficulty even feeding a large swath of the population it is hard to imagine a day when everyone will own computers with voice-recognition software.

It takes time to learn how to type well, but there's a payoff. The ability to type well is empowering. But it's more than just being a fast typist. Accuracy is essential.

For home school teachers who want to help their children become faster and better on a keyboard, there are plenty of software programs that can assist. Do a little research first, though. Make sure it's compatible with your operating system. And, if available, read reviews of others' experiences, especially with tech support if a complication should come up. There are also free online tutorials that don't require a download.

I myself am grateful that my mom had me take that typing class in high school. (My mom recently told me there were three things she wanted her four boys to learn while young that she wished she had learned: how to swim, how to drive and how to type.) I received my first type-writer as a graduation present. Even if typewriters are dinosaurs now, mine proved invaluable when I attended college. To this day I love the QWERTY keyboard.

. . . .

Chapter 5: Research Skills

Sometimes, research projects can be overwhelming. An abundance of information on whatever your student's interested in is available via the Internet, libraries, and books. Furthermore, once they've picked the perfect topic, it's easy to stagnate because the student doesn't know where to begin. In this chapter, we'll talk about a few strategies for navigating through all this information, and methods for gathering appropriate information.

First of all, there's a great type of human called "The Librarian" whose job is researching. In the past, librarians mainly organized books and dealt out fines. These days, with digital catalogues and the opportunities to gather information expanding so rapidly, their job has changed a bit. The librarian today is less the old-fashioned matron shushing the loud and more of a hip info curator who excels at employing various digital tools to organize and disseminate information. Instead of primarily categorizing books, the librarian is now responsible for overseeing Internet use. Along with this changing job description comes a new set of skills. The specific librarian skills that are appropriate for this conversation are the ability to assess the value of web pages and skill at navigating online databases in order to find valuable, relevant, and reliable information. In other words, your local librarian, in addition to being a friendly face, will be well qualified to help you navigate the Internet to find information that you seek for your research project.

You can also access these same resources by yourself. There are some excellent academic databases online, with compilations of all sorts of academic articles and abstracts, much like the card catalogue of a library. These databases tend to be organized according to topic. For example, PubChem is an online database that mainly organizes articles on the topic of chemistry, while Academic OneFile is a multidisciplinary database. Unfortunately, not all online databases are accessible for free. A Google search of "list of academic databases" will provide a few starting points. After you've reviewed these resources, you can figure out which ones work best for your particular needs. While it may be tedious to find an article that is spot-on perfect for your research project, you can be confident that the information found in these databases is trustworthy.

In addition to finding information in academic databases, you can take an old-fashioned trip to the library. Books are full of information about all sorts of topics. Be sure to research the expertise of the author and cross-reference the facts presented to ensure accuracy.

The Internet is easiest way to access information, but it is also prone to misinformation. While using the Internet to search for sources, it's important to make sure your information is accurate, appropriate, and attributed.

Because of its clear organization and easy navigation, Wikipedia has become a popular online resource, but here's a word of caution. While Wikipedia has greatly improved its fact-checking and fact-contribution methods, it can still contain false or disputed information. I recommend using Wikipedia as a tool to get a general idea for your topic. It is also a great source for further information because Wikipedia includes links to other sources where their information came from. So, start at Wiki-pedia to get a general idea and use it as a launching pad to find more information on other sites. Don't forget to check the credibility of those sites, too.

Many people posting on the Internet can't necessarily be trusted. Consider the number of blogs and websites that require no verifica-tion to publish information. While widely read websites are held ac-countable for producing accurate and appropriate information, most websites are not. It is important to know how to differentiate between websites that provide reliable information and websites that do not. While there's no sure-fire way to wean the good from the bad, these tricks can help you navigate this sea of information:

- Never quote a website if you can't identify the author, unless you know the source is credible.

- Consider the motivation of the author or website. Is the LoveForests Federation writing about a company that will replace acres of forest with an airport or a used car lot? If so, they may be biased.

- Consider the timeliness of the webpage or article. An article from 1995 might be accurate if your topic hasn't changed much since then, such as a discussion about the battle of Gettysburg. On the other hand, an article from 1995 about computers will definitely be dated.

- Consider the audience when compiling information. The same statistic might be more meaningful to a particular audience if quoted from one source rather than another. For example, if you're writing a research paper about car seats, a mother may want your article to focus on safety, while a baby would be interested in reading about car seats in terms of comfort. (O.K., so we know babies can't read, but you get the idea.)

After you've searched the academic databases, talked to the librarian, checked out a stack of books from the library, and found a few websites that provide relevant and reliable information, you're ready to write your research paper. Remember, though, that it is very important to talk about where you found the information. This habit both protects you from most consequences of reporting bad information and plagiarism. Even if you checked the website thoroughly, it could still have given you bad information.

Chapter 6: Attribution

Beginning writing students often fall into the plagiarism sinkhole—most often unintentionally. Inexperience is usually the culprit. Unfortunately, inexperience doesn't justify plagiarism. Every student needs to practice citing the sources they use until it's a habit. Once it's a habit, they can face the world with the necessary tools to feel confident about the material they present.

It's a natural and vital learning experience for young students to borrow ideas from great thinkers and writers. In fact, it would be completely erroneous, and a tad pretentious, to claim that a new idea doesn't have some basis in previous thought. The learning experience doesn't end with borrowing ideas, however; the student also needs to learn how to give credit where it's due. In other words, to cite his or her sources.

"Source citations" might sound complicated and daunting, but it doesn't have to be. In fact, if the student can recognize which material he is borrowing and include the important information about where he found it, he is developing good habits that will help him throughout his academic career.

You might be confused about what types of material require attribution. Is it only exact quotes? What about paraphrased material or information that is well-known to a specific group of people but not known generally? Or what about statistics from a census or poll, for example? The truth is, everything that is not original material created by the student requires attribution. This includes quotes, statistics, paraphrased material, borrowed ideas, and information not known generally. If any steps have to be taken to look up or verify material, it should be attributed. And, let's face it, attention and care put into attribution in the first place will can potentially save a lot of pain in dealing with accusations of plagiarism later.

How that material is attributed, though, is a little more flexible. Usually, each particular field of writing has a unique attribution style that includes the most important information in a relevant order. For example, the three most commonly used citation styles are MLA (Modern Language Association), Chicago Style, and APA (American Psychological Association). English departments usually use MLA, communication and journalism programs usually use Chicago style. APA is often used in social sciences such as education or linguistics (Yuan). Typically, students just beginning their writing career don't know which citation style they will most frequently use throughout their lives. Thus, it doesn't matter which one you choose. After the students develop the strong habit of citing borrowed material, they will find it easier to transition between citation styles. In the meantime, it will benefit the student to cultivate the habit of using any citation style.

While citation styles may differ some with respect to required information, all styles include basic information that helps identify the original source, and where it can be found again. Contrary to what you may be thinking, the process of citing sources isn't used solely for the purpose of catching students plagiarizing. Source citations are primarily for the engrossed reader who is very interested in the student's paper and wants to know more. Often, all that's needed in the original text is the author's last name, with the rest of the information appended in a "works cited" page. For example, you probably noticed that I included an in-text citation referencing Yuan, the author of the webpage where I found the information about which academic disciplines use which citation styles. MLA requires information in this general format:

> Editor, author, or compiler name (if available). Name of Site. Version number. Name of institution/organization affiliated with the site (sponsor or publisher), date of resource creation (if available). Medium of publication. Date of access.

Thus, using MLA, the rest of the information will look like this:

> Yuan, Bright. Getting Help with Citation Style. UCLA Graduate Writing Center, 2007-2009. Web. March 25, 2013.

Many resources are available to help teachers and students learn to attribute without anxiety, including reference books and online resources. With these tools, students will learn to cite correctly and easily avoid plagiarism pitfalls.

Chapter 7: The Writing Schedule

It's my conviction that a heavy homework load can be a burden on students to such an extent that they only have one objective: to finish as quickly as possible and be done with it. Learning how to write well is different. It is not a quiz with right and wrong answers. It is not about answers at all. It is about a process of deliberation and problem solving. How do I convey what I am thinking in the most effective and interesting way so that someone actually wants to read it?

Consequently, the exercises in this small volume are not intended to be whisked through as quickly as possible. We suggest one exercise a week. This means meeting twice a week. In the first part of the week meet with each student to review the writing assignment to ensure he or she understands. Later in the week, meet to review the work. The latter is a private meeting with each student individually.

You can see from this kind of regimen the advantage home school has over public school writing classes. Teachers would be overwhelmed if they had to find time to meet individually with each student on every assignment. Yet the process of coming alongside and collaborating with the student to help improve his or her written expression will engender more satisfying results and will produce more effective communications.

As for the students' writing schedules, encourage them to find their own time and space for writing. Some will sit at the table during school hours. Others may want to curl up in a hammock under the open sky or in your favorite easy chair while you're in the yard or at the office.

Chapter 8: Grading the Work

For what it's worth, I do not have teaching degrees. Nor do I have any scientific studies to back my teaching approach. Everything here stems from personal observation regarding my own experiences as a student, a parent and a reader, with a dose of applied critical thinking a.k.a. common sense.

By grading, I mean the process of working alongside the student and conveying your observations, corrections and encouragement. Grading your student's writing is probably the most important part of the teaching process. Going over the assignment together gives you an opportunity to engage the mind of your child or student and should always be done privately, one on one. First off, criticism and correction can be painful enough when done privately, so doing it in front of others, whether siblings or classmates, can be especially so.

It does not have to be time consuming, but it does require taking the time to sit together and go over the work.

When I was young I had a supervisor who believed one should say ten positive things to a person before saying something negative. He was always concerned that criticism would discourage employees rather than help. No employee is without shortcomings, neither will your student's writing be.

That is why my approach to grading involves a variety of criterion so that one can give high marks on aspects of the work, which serve to soften the critical comments. In our home I used the following criterion when evaluating work:

Creativity
Originality
Accuracy
Spelling
Grammar
Punctuation
Neatness

I always gave encouragement when our kids became emotionally engaged or psychologically involved in their work. Praise aggressively when you see this. This praise is very important because the first thing writers of all ages notice are those red marks. Those blemishes can breed discouragement. This is why I start each grading session by grading intangibles like creativity and originality.

As already noted, when students are writing essays, articles or stories I try to place myself "alongside" them so I'm on their team as they attempt to communicate an idea or feeling. I ask questions like, "Is this really what you meant? Would another word help describe that better? Would re-organizing these sentences produce a stronger statement? Can you tell me why you chose to end it this way?"

Spelling, grammar, punctuation and neatness all need proper attention, and by keeping the student motivated to write, you create ample opportunities to resolve all these technical aspects of their work.

Chapter 9: Tone, Rhythm and Creating Interest

Anyone can write sentences. Creating sentences that make other people want to read more is another thing altogether. The best writing requires cultivating a level of sensitivity to tone, rhythm and stylistic elements.

Whether writing stories or essays, interest can be amplified by giving attention to the opening lines. Interest is sustained by a variety of techniques as well as a sensitivity to pacing. The exercises here aim to sow seeds and give the student ideas that can be fertilized and nurtured.

Attention to detail is an important part of developing excellence in any discipline. I'm fond of repeating John Gardner's maxim, "Detail is the lifeblood of fiction."

Throughout the exercises my hope is to engage minds, to challenge children to become better observers and thinkers. Perhaps you yourself will become a better observer through the exercises here, in which case this slim volume is having a double-benefit.

One of the problems young writers have is the tendency to overdo it when trying to create an emotion, whether tension or passion or fear. Exclamation points abound in bad writing. Do not let your student overdo it! Yet, despite the "tiresome acrobatics" and "flashy effects" that Katherine Anne Porter warns against, occasionally it's perfectly acceptable to break the rules. Someone once wrote an entire novel without using the letter e. He must have been told it couldn't be done. (I wonder if it's now available as an eBook.)

All that to say this: you can expect some fairly over-the-top writing at times. If you're able to reign it in without discouraging these explorations, you're doing well. For now, don't be too harsh. Their current exuberance will give you opportunities to review their spelling, punctuation and grammar. If the habit persists, you may try gently asking, "Is it your intention to come across here like you're shouting?" A lot of times we're not aware of how we're coming across.

One more word of caution. In music it's possible to be tone deaf and unable to carry a tune. It's my belief that how sentences sound is as important as the grammar and content. This will be a problem for the student who is unable to "hear" the clunkiness of their language. Don't dwell on it. Not every student aspires to be the next Pulitzer Prize winner, just as not every athlete will becomes a superstar in the NFL. That doesn't prevent kids from playing football after school and enjoying it.

Don't overthink it. Make it fun and it's possible you'll see miracles.

Chapter 10: Recommended Books

- Strunk & White. *The Elements of Style.*

  Of this essential writer's tool the St. Paul Pioneer Press writes, "This excellent book, which should go off to college with every freshman, is recognized as the best book of its kind we have."

- William Zinsser. *On Writing Well.*

  A book with sound advice regarding the basics of writing well. More than a million copies have been sold because it tells how to write with clarity and effectiveness. I know at least one writer who re-reads it every year.

- Quinn, Arthur. *Figures of Speech.*

  Another practical book that gives an overview of the most common figures of speech, with examples of each. You don't have to memorize them, just know that they exist, and that sometimes when you break the rules they even have a name for it.

Reference Materials:

- Either *Roget's Thesaurus* or *Rodale's Synonym Finder.*

  Each is helpful for finding alternative words. Online substitutes exist. Thesaurus.com should be bookmarked in every writer's browser.

- A good dictionary (both a hard copy and an Internet reference)

- Some type of citation guide (either a hard copy or an Internet reference site) See: www.bucknell.edu/x91350.xml

- *A Dictionary of Modern American Usage*, by Brian A. Garner

PART II:
The Exercises

Exercise 1: Quickie Descriptions

Take 15 minutes to write answers to the following in your writing notebook.

1. Describe what it feels like to wake up in the morning.
   (Or, how did you feel when you awoke this morning?)

2. How many words do you know that mean "BIG"? List them.

3. Imagine something you have never seen. What would you name it and why?

4. If you had three wishes, and one was for you, one for someone else, and one for all people, what wishes would you make?

5. If you had a magic carpet, where would you go and what would you do when you got there?

6. Write a short dialogue between you and an animal. Use proper punctuation.

Exercise 2: Quickie Descriptions

Take 15 minutes to write answers to the following in your writing notebook. Use complete sentences (i.e. no phrases). Use proper punctuation.

1. In one paragraph, describe what it feels like if outside.

2. Imagine a new kind of tree. What is this tree like? What is it called? What kind of fruit or leaves does it have? Write two to four sentences about this new tree.

3. Write a dialogue with two or more people who are happy. Do not use the words like "happy" or "joy" or "cheerful". Also, try to show their happiness by describing their faces and actions.

Exercise 3: Quickie Descriptions

Take 15 minutes to write answers to the following in your writing notebook. Use complete sentences (i.e. no phrases). Use proper punctuation.

1. (Using stronger verbs.) Write a paragraph about something you saw somewhere at the mall, downtown or at the lake. It could be a person, something that happened, a display, or a whole room full of things. Avoid using the words "is", "was", or other variations of the "be" verb.

2. (Imagination exercise) If people had a third eye, where should it be and why? What would it see?

3. Write a list of words that describe various shades of blue. Write at least five. (Extra point for each extra word above five.)

4. (Observation) Write five statements about one of your pets. Write a paragraph using the information in these five statements. (If you do not have a pet, choose your mother, father, sister or brother.)

Exercise 4: Discovering & Using New Words

Sometimes our writing is less interesting because we use the same words over and over again. One way to inject new life into our vocabulary is to read through the dictionary. The sheer number of words is amazing.

Your assignment is to skim through the dictionary and find ten interesting one-syllable words that you normally do not use, that might add spice to a story. Make sentences using each word.
(Note: Try to use words that begin with different letters of the alphabet.)

Purpose of the assignment: To show that you do not need to use BIG words to have interesting words in your writing.

Exercise 5: Varying Sentence Length

One of the keys to dynamic, engaging writing is to use different kinds of words, different kinds of sentences, and varying sentence length. Here's your assignment. Write a scene from a story. Use both short and long sentences. Use different kinds of sentences.

(Do you know what I mean by this? Great!) Most of all, make it interesting and have fun.

Exercise 6: Perspective

Stories can be told from many different points of view. *First person* is when you write from the point of view of one person who tells the story: "I was walking to school one day, when suddenly..."

Second person is rare, but writers sometimes use it. "You were walking to school when suddenly a car flew out of control and almost hit you. Fortunately, you leaped behind a tree and..."

Third person is most common. "He walked to school with his head down, kicking a stone as he walked along. Suddenly..."

Third person enables the writer to tell about many things that the main character doesn't know about, allowing the reader to follow many different scenes at once. In *first person* you generally learn everything in the story through one person's senses.

Some stories are told from what is called the *third person* limited perspective, writing about one character and limiting the viewpoint of the reader by covering the story as if it is *first person*, except it's written in *third person*. The best way to understand this is by contrasting it with *third person* omniscient. Omniscient means "all-knowing" and in that perspective the storyteller has the ability to show what all the various characters are thinking and feeling. In *third person* limited, the reader knows what the main character knows.

Your assignment is to write the same one-page story two different ways, using a different perspective in each. For extra credit you can write one page in each of the above four voices.

Note: Try to use long and short sentences. Make the opening interesting. Please check your spelling and punctuation. Be creative, and have fun.

Exercise 7: Quoting Others – Part One

One way to strengthen your speeches, essays, articles, and editorials is to use quotes from famous people. Their significance adds authority to your ideas. Many great speakers quote others who went before them as a way to indicate that their ideas are shared by history. It is important that when you quote someone else, directly or as a paraphrase, you must give credit to that person and not pretend it was your own idea. This is called "attribution," which means that you properly attribute the original source of the statement.

Your assignment is to choose a famous quote and write a paragraph about what it teaches.

Exercise 8: Quoting Others – Part Two

Choose one of the following quotes about history and write a paragraph about what it means. You may use the Internet to research first.

History abhors determinism but cannot tolerate chance.
~ Bernard de Voto

The subject of history is the life of peoples and of humanity. To catch and pin down in words -- that is, to describe directly the life, not only of humanity, but even of a single people – appears to be impossible.
~ Leo Tolstoy

Human history is in essence a history of ideas.
~ H. G. Wells

Advice to persons about to write history: Don't.
~ Lord Acton

What experience and history teach is this: that people and governments never have learned anything from history, or acted on principles deduced from it.
~ G.W.F. Hegel

A people without history is like the wind on the buffalo grass.
~ Sioux saying

The health of nations is more important than the wealth of nations.
~ Will Durant

Exercise 9: Understanding Concepts

Write one to two paragraphs about a topic. State your topic. Use a famous saying or a quote from the Book of Proverbs* in your paragraph. If you can, give an example from life to illustrate.

You can choose any topic you want. If you can't think of a topic, choose a topic from among the following.

Pride
Loyalty
Frugality
Creativity
Courage
Recklessness
Foolishness
Humility
Flattery
Talkativeness
Stubbornness
Wisdom
Sincerity
Friendship
Honesty
Gratefulness
Humor
Excellence
Learning
Problem Solving

*The Book of Proverbs (also called the Proverbs of Solomon) is located after the Psalms in the Hebrew Bible or what is known as the Christian Old Testament. Chapters 10 through 31 are especially rich with short, pithy sayings that deal with character and wisdom.

Exercise 10: Dialogue and Imagination

Write a one-page dialogue with two or more characters beginning with the statement, "In the name of the King I command you to open this gate!"

Idea starters and advice

Before you begin, use a separate sheet of paper to name your characters and define them. Jot notes describing them. You may even want to find pictures in a magazine of your characters… or draw them. Once you clearly see the characters and the "story," begin to write.

You will be graded for spelling, grammar, punctuation, interest and originality. Punctuation is most important. Please pay attention to details and write neatly.

Exercise 11: The PIN Method

The PIN Method was developed by Dr. Edward DeBono to help people develop their critical thinking skills. Dr. DeBono taught that everything has a Positive, Interesting, and Negative aspect.

For example: There was frost on the ground the other night.

A Positive thing about this might be that mom loves the fall. The first frost is part of the process that changes the leaves and makes the trees so beautiful in this part of the country.

An Interesting thing might be to think about how the moisture in the air becomes ice crystals, and to think about why clear cloudless skies produce hard frosts.

A Negative thing might be that the first frost tells us summer is passing, and many people enjoy swimming and freedom from school. Also, winter is nearer now, and with it, snow.

Your writing assignment this week is to find an article, editorial or letter to the editor in the newspaper and apply the PIN Method to it. Briefly summarize what it says (one paragraph) and then write a positive, interesting and negative observation about it.

Exercise 12: Book Review

Write a review of a book you have read in the past six months. Answer the following questions:

1. Who wrote it? If you know anything about the author, write a short paragraph about him or her. If you do not, go online and research. Write a paragraph about what you learned. Use your own words.

2. What is the book about? 1-2 paragraphs.

3. Why do you think the author wrote this book? (One sentence is OK and you can guess. You may also write more than a sentence.)

4. What did you like most about the book?

5. What did you like least about the book?

6. Is there anything else you would like to say about the book?

Exercise 13: Word Usage – Part One

Using words properly.

Write sentences using each of the following words:

feasible
ache
decent
descent
schedule
either
ether
accuse
hypocrite
prefer
compliment
complement

Exercise 14: Word Usage – Part Two

Learning to recognize quality writing.

Find an especially interesting sentence in one of the books you are reading or have read recently. Write the sentence in your notebook and then explain why you chose this sentence. What makes this sentence interesting to you? (Extra points if you can list at least three things and write a short paragraph about each one.)

Exercise 15: Description and Observation

Pick someone we know and describe their features so that we know who it is, but don't reveal their name or how we know them. Use as much detail as possible.

Additional Instructions

1. Use at least one metaphor.

2. If possible, use long and short sentences in your descriptions.

3. Try to write a full page of description.

Tip One: Begin by making a list of observations on a separate piece of paper and then when you write the description of this person, combine some of the observations.

Tip Two: Think of the questions that you can answer like who, what, when, where, how and why. How do they talk? How do they eat? How do they interact with others? Where do they spend their free time? What do they like? Who are their friends?

Ask your OWN set of questions, and write answers. Then, write your description in the notebook. The more questions you can create and answer, the more detail you have to work with.

Tip Three: Have fun

Exercise 16: Imagination and Observation

Choose a room in your house that you would like to describe. Now, describe it from the point of view of being one inch tall. Go ahead. What do you see? Write one full page of description.

Afterword

Do I Speak In Vain?

If I should speak, who would hear?

A multitude of countless voices droning, shrieking, badgering, insisting, whispering, flaunting, haunting, announcing, trouncing, reflecting, directing, telling, selling, impressing, distressing, helping, hurting, assisting, confusing, clarifying, obscuring... sharing ideas, feelings, concepts, truth, and even madness.

Is it foolishness?

To be one more voice, insignificant as a drop of rain in the Rocky Mountains, for one vain moment dashing pitifully into the massive granite heart of a continent. A continent! One drop, exploding in useless splendor, colliding with a whole continent set in its ways. Is this not the ultimate futility?

Perhaps.

But then again... Perhaps there is a waiting seed, expectant, hungering, thirsting, languishing for that single drop, that drop of nourishment, to gain sufficient strength to break free from the confines of its tiny prison shell of self, to burst asunder through earth and darkness, into life. And my single drop, finding its mark, is not spilled in vain. As this seedling to sapling grows, it reaches up to grasp gloriously in daily snatches the light of life, rejoicing now that it, too, can fulfill its destiny and purpose in being.

This is why I write.

Appendix A: 101 Writing Prompts

I believe it beneficial to spend time writing every day. It doesn't have to be formal or require much editing. 15-20 minutes writing one page about a familiar topic. Or, they can easily make something up. These exercises can be in different categories, emphasizing different skills, like persuasive writing, informative writing or creative writing. For example: "Write one page about which is better: books or tablets."

These exercises can be performed either on a computer or in your writing notebooks. If you use a computer, make a different document for each exercise. If you write in your notebook, one page is sufficient for each, but the student may write more if he or she wishes.

1. Describe something you can see that's green.
2. Explain how to catch a bus.
3. Describe a sunset.
4. Describe hearing to a deaf person.
5. Which do you like more, peanut butter or chocolate, and why?
6. Do you like dancing? Why or why not?
7. Compare and contrast a mountain and a snow bank.
8. Design a new air conditioning system that does not use electricity.
9. Make a list of the benefits of having only three fingers.
10. Describe a foreign country that you would like to visit some day.
11. Which is better, a shovel or an axe?

Dialogue Topics

12. Write a page of conversation between a toaster and a piece of toast.
13. Write a page of conversation between a dentist and a ten-year-old boy or girl.
14. Write a page of conversation between two meatballs.

15. Write a page of conversation between two aliens visiting Kansas for the first time.

16. Write a page of dialogue between the Tin Man and the Cowardly Lion in the Wizard of Oz. (If you have not seen the movie, then write a page of dialogue between a lion and a hippo.)

17. Write a page of dialogue between two dust particles.

18. Write a page of dialogue between two items in a kitchen.

More Prompts

19. Create a new word and define it. Talk about it in detail and use it in a few sentences.

20. Create a new game. What do you need to play and what are the rules?

21. Explain how to use a rolling pin.

22. Create an organization whose acronym is EDRT. What do they do and what are their meetings like?

23. What is your favorite color? What would it be like if everything was your favorite color?

24. Write about an old lady giving a dog treat to a dog, first from the perspective of the dog, and then from the perspective of the old lady.

25. Interview your favorite musician.

26. Who is your favorite author and why? (Extra point if it's Ed Newman.)

27. What does it feel like to have a mustache?

28. Write a page of ideas about energy.

29. Give directions on how to get to the nearest _____ (Fill in the blank. Make it complicated.)

30. Write about something that makes you happy.

31. They say a picture is worth a thousand words. Unfortunately we lost your family photo and you need to describe it for us now.

32. Write a short story in which jumping saved your life.

33. Describe a scene from your favorite movie including details about characters, setting, plot and dialogue.

Persuasion

34. Write a short essay persuading us to move to your favorite place in the world.
35. Persuade your parents to bring you to McDonald's tonight.
36. Your parents are bringing you to McDonald's. Persuade them to take you somewhere else.
37. Persuade a troll to let you pass by on the bridge without having to pay the toll.
38. Persuade a cat to stop playing with his food.

Miscellaneous Topics

39. What are the positive and negative things about advertising? How does advertising help people? How does advertising hurt people?
40. What will life be like in 50 years when you are an older person?
41. In what ways do our bodies change when we get older and why?
42. How has the Internet changed our lives?
43. What would it be like to live in the Arctic Circle?
44. What are some of the ways farming is important today?
45. What are some of the ways volunteers play a role in society?
46. Choose a wild animal. What is it like to have it as your pet? How do you take care of it? What is your life like?
47. Dolphins are considered very intelligent. What is it like to be an intelligent creature that lived all its life in the ocean?
48. What would your life be like if you lived in the jungle 4,000 years ago?
49. In which time period would you most like to live and why?
50. What would it be like to live in a cave?
51. Share everything you know about trees. Then see what else you can learn about trees through online research. Share that here, too.
52. Who is your favorite artist and why?
53. Write a short synopsis of your favorite book.
54. What country would you like to visit before you die and what would you like to do there?

55. Do you have a favorite planet? What would it be like to live there?

56. What is your favorite kind of car? Describe it in as much detail as you can, including its color, shape and history. Where would you like to drive it? Describe your road trip.

57. What would it be like to fly an airplane? Where would you fly it? What kind of plane would you find most exciting to fly, an old-style bi-plane or a modern jet, and why?

58. If you had to be an insect, what would you become and what would a typical day be like?

59. You are one of the deckhands on the Nina, Pinta or Santa Maria when Columbus crossed the Atlantic and discovered America. Write a page as if it were a diary entry. It can be the first day, a middle day or the last day of the journey.

60. Choose a product or service and tell how you would market or advertise it. What would your slogan be in your advertising? How would you tell people what your business was about?

61. What kinds of lessons have your learned from your parents? What are some lessons you have learned from your friends?

62. Do we have too many people in the world?

63. Do we have too much crime? What can we do about it?

64. What would life be like without money?

65. Does our country place too much emphasis on sports? Why do people like sports so much?

66. What is your favorite sport and why? (or if you do not have one, why or why not?)

67. What would life be like without music?

Rules and Stories

68. Write five rules for sending a letter.

69. Write three rules that you think would make people happier.

70. Write a short story about how a man or woman helped someone.

71. Write a short story about a dog that saved someone's life.

72. Write a short story about flying in a balloon.

73. Write a short story about a seagull on a big adventure.

74. Write a list of 10 more things you would like to write about.

Compare and Contrast

75. Day and Night
76. North and South
77. Summer and Winter
78. Monkeys and Tigers
79. New York and Los Angeles
80. Iowa and Colorado
81. Trumpets and Trombones
82. Beethoven and the Beatles
83. Television and Theater
84. If you were stuck on a deserted island and could only have three books with you, what would they be and why? One page description of the three books.
85. What are the pros and cons of government funded public education?
86. What are the pros and cons of oil as a source of energy in the U.S.?
87. Do you like to cook? Why? What is the recipe for your favorite meal?
88. What are the best ways to teach children manners? What manners are especially important and why?
89. Describe one of the worst experiences that ever happened to you and what did you learn from that experience?
90. Why is cooperation important? Describe one or some experiences of collaboration in your life?
91. Describe the plot of your favorite movie and why it so impressed you?
92. What is your favorite kind of food and what is your least favorite? Why?
93. What is the difference between Fast Food restaurant food and fresh food from the garden?
94. What are the qualities that make a leader a leader?
95. What is a balanced diet and why is it important?
96. World hunger is a serious problem. How can we solve it?

97. If you had been the first man to walk on the moon, how would you describe this experience? What did you feel? What did you see? What were your goals?

98. Your older brother went off to fight in the Civil War. How did you feel when he came back alive? Write a story or two that he told you about the battles he was in?

99. It is 1849. Your dad left home to go to California during the Gold Rush but never came back. Tell us what happened to him? How did it affect your mom? How did it affect you?

100. Write a page about your favorite hobby? Why do you like this? If you couldn't do that as a hobby what would you be doing?

101. What are the pros and cons of small towns and big cities?

EdNote: *There are a number of books featuring writing prompts at Amazon.com or in many book stores. You can also find writing prompts online at www.reddit.com/r/WritingPrompts/top/*

Warning to Parents: *A few of these may not be suitable for younger children.*

Appendix B: The Seven Laws of Teaching

A book that I believe is most useful for teachers is *The Seven Laws of Teaching*, by John Milton Gregory. Published in 1884, it is still relevant today.

Gregory's book is a straightforward, clear presentation of the seven principles of teaching. He also outlines the five levels of learning. Rote memorization is not the ultimate aim of schooling. Yes, it's nice to know a few facts of history now and then, but an education is more than knowing stats, dates and data.

Gregory affirms, "Knowing comes by thinking, not by being told." The key to success in life and career is applied critical thinking. This is why the real goal of these exercises is to turn a light bulb on inside our students' heads, to create opportunities for engagement, to waken the mind and help young people get past the notion of "correct answers" for the sake of a grade.

It's been my hope that my *Writing Exercises* achieves the same outcome.

Acknowledgements

This book was actually my wife Susie's idea. On Thursday June 10, 2004, after dinner at the Maya, a Mexican restaurant here in Duluth, Susie said I should write a book called *Writing Exercises*. She had been reviewing some papers related to our years of homeschooling and came across a folder with writing assignments that I had created to teach writing to our son and daughter.

My goal in creating these exercises had been to make writing something the kids would actually look forward to. Honesty forces me to admit that Christina probably enjoyed writing a bit more than Micah, but both of them showed a marked enthusiasm when the bug got into them, and both produced very imaginative, well-constructed stories, essays and writing fragments. And both became better writers through the experience.

By the time she was twelve Christina already had two original short stories published, each showing a fairly high level of sophistication for a child that age. (If I may quote my Kentucky-born grandmother, "Now I hain't braggin', ya hear?")

Writing is one of those magical skills that not only enables us to communicate with others, it also helps us understand ourselves. Writing forces us to clarify our thoughts. As our language becomes more precise in the reflection of our thoughts, feelings and observations, we get better at articulating our innermost selves. Once writing well begins to matter to us, we're forced to think with greater care about the words we choose, and the nuances of language. It makes us better people.

Children who develop good writing skills will find their school work easier, both high school and college. They will also become more effective communicators. Even if your son grows up to become the strong silent type, he'll still be able to write eloquent love notes or conscientious complaints.

Ultimately, in some small way it is my hope that these exercises will help pupils learn how to recognize and appreciate good writing, and in so doing become readers for a lifetime.

. . . .

This book would not have been possible without assistance from a variety of people. Thank you to Professor David Beard of the University of Minnesota-Duluth for reviewing an early version of this manuscript and suggesting ways to improve its usefulness. Thanks, also, to Grace Moores, a journalism student whose assistance helped provide additional direction to the first part of this book, including contributions to the chapters on handwriting, attribution, research and the writer's notebook. A nod to John Baker who helped edit the book, improving it significantly, and to Jeff Spry for designing the cover and producing the layout.

Finally, a big thanks to James Nickel, the wise friend, author and mathematics teacher who shared *The Seven Laws of Teaching* with me 35 years ago.

. . . .

I invite you to follow me on Twitter @ennyman3 and my Ennyman's Territory blog, http://pioneerproductions.blogspot.com/

If you enjoyed this book and found value in it, please leave a review on Amazon.com. Here are some other books by Ed Newman.

Reflections from the North Country, 2007 – 2015

Notes, observations and impressions about the music, art and life of the Northland's Bob Dylan

Reflections is a compilation of all my Dylan-themed blog posts from 2007 to December 2015. Available on loan from the Duluth Public Library.

A Remarkable Tale from the Land of Podd

A Children's Picture Book

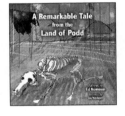

Illustrated by Ian Welshons, *A Remarkable Tale from the Land of Podd* uses wry humor, rhyme, and captivating illustrations to teach an important lesson about self- awareness and self-worth. No matter how we perceive ourselves, we can make a difference.

Ideal for children in 1st through 4th grade, though engaging for all ages.

The Red Scorpion

A Young Adult Novel

A haunted house story with a supernatural twist. Lord of the Flies meets Stephen King. One Amazon reviewer called it "a good mystery/suspense/science fiction thriller... carefully crafted and realistically portrayed." One reader wrote, "This book kept me reading straight through till the end. It kept me guessing and wondering what would happen next." Just like a good story should.

Available as an eBook at Amazon.com ($2.99)

Intergalactica

In the spring of 2012 I was involved in an exhilarating collaborative art project called Artist Kamikaze IV. Intergalactica is an eBook version of our project in story form. Available free on iTunes at:

https://itunes.apple.com/us/book/intergalactica/
id687348057?mt=11&ls=1

Short Story Collections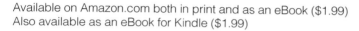

Unremembered Histories

The paranormal becomes the common denominator in these six original stories. An Amazon.com reviewer wrote, "If you value the short-story form, written in a way that entertains, informs, and prompts you to think, then there's a lot to appreciate in this little gem." In the 1990's one of my favorite stories, Duel of the Poets, was translated into Croatian to be a cornerstone for a poetry site there.

Available on Amazon.com both in print and as an eBook ($1.99)
Also available as an eBook for Kindle ($1.99)

Newmanesque

Newmanesque is my second collection of original short fiction. This set of stories includes The M Zone, A Poem About Truth, The Unfinished Stories of Richard Allen Garston, The Nose, and Terrorists Preying, which has been translated into French by Aude Fondard. One reader of these stories wrote, "My very first impression is that there's a certain style in some ways similar to Franz Kafka which is good and intense... very mysterious for one doesn't know where the whole thing is going to go, but it's sure that there's a message to be captured from the many moments stated in the short sentences that are all poignant to the story."

Available as an eBook at Amazon.com ($0.99)

The Breaking Point and Other Stories

My third collection of short stories features my winning 1991 Arrowhead Regional Fiction Competition story "The Breaking Point" plus four other stories. One reader wrote that the stories "contain insight into relationships" with "subject matter regarding love relationship's emotions, expectations, illusions, and delusions..." In the midst of ordinary lives there can be decisive extraordinary events.

Available as an eBook at Amazon.com ($1.99)

Made in the USA
Middletown, DE
23 August 2017